MATH FOR
MINECRAFTERS

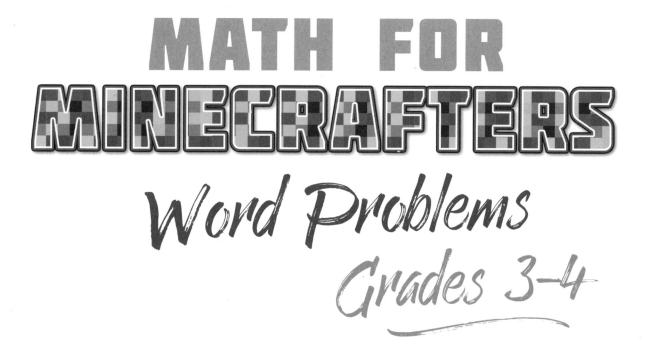

Word Problems

Grades 3-4

Illustrated by Amanda Brack

Sky Pony Press
New York

Sky Pony Press books may be purchased in bulk at special discounts for sales promotion, corporate gifts, fund-raising, or educational purposes. Special editions can also be created to specifications. For details, contact the Special Sales Department, Sky Pony Press, 307 West 36th Street, 11th Floor, New York, NY 10018 or info@skyhorsepublishing.com.

Sky Pony® is a registered trademark of Skyhorse Publishing, Inc.®, a Delaware corporation.

Visit our website at www.skyponypress.com.

Authors, books, and more at SkyPonyPressBlog.com.

10 9 8 7 6 5 4 3 2 1

Library of Congress Cataloging-in-Publication Data is available on file.

Cover design by Brian Peterson

Cover illustration by Bill Greenhead

Book design by Kevin Baier

Print ISBN: 978-1-5107-3086-1

Printed in Canada

A NOTE TO PARENTS

When you want to reinforce classroom skills at home, it's crucial to have kid-friendly learning materials. This *Math for Minecrafters* workbook transforms math practice into an irresistible adventure complete with diamond swords, zombies, skeletons, and creepers. That means less arguing over homework and more fun overall.

Math for Minecrafters is also fully aligned with National Common Core Standards for 3rd- and 4th-grade math. What does that mean, exactly? All of the problems in this book correspond to what your child is expected to learn in school. This eliminates confusion and builds confidence for greater homework-time success!

As the workbook progresses, the word problems become more advanced. Encourage your child to progress at his or her own pace. Learning is best when students are challenged, but not frustrated. What's most important is that your Minecrafter is engaged in his or her own learning.

Whether it's the joy of seeing their favorite game characters on every page or the thrill of solving challenging problems just like Steve and Alex, there is something in this workbook to entice even the most reluctant math student.

Happy adventuring!

MULTIPLYING ONE-DIGIT NUMBERS

Read the problem carefully. Use the pictures for extra help. Write the answer in the space provided.

1. You meet 8 skeletons and each one shoots 7 arrows at you. How many arrows are shot in all?

2. You are attacked by 6 groups of 4 silverfish. How many silverfish are attacking in all?

3. A ghast shoots 10 fireballs at you. A group of 3 more ghasts approaches and each ghast shoots 2 fireballs at you. How many fireballs are shot at you in all?

4. 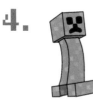 You see 10 creepers. You get 3 unit of gunpowder from each of them. How many unit of gunpowder do you get in all?

5. You find 7 shulkers in an End temple. You take 4 damage from each of them. How much damage do you take in all?

6. You place 3 torches on each of 3 cave walls. How many torches do you place?

7. You brew 4 potions of Leaping and each one restores 2 hearts. How many hearts can be restored with 8 potions of Leaping?

8. You start your game with 9 shovels in your inventory. You have 3 times as many swords in your inventory. How many swords do you have?

9. You encounter 6 groups of 7 cave spiders. How many spiders do you encounter?

10. You destroy a bunch of zombies and collect 5 pieces of rotten flesh. If you collect this much rotten flesh 3 times in one day, how many pieces of rotten flesh do you collect in all?

11. To make one golden sword, you need 2 gold ingots. If you want to make 8 golden swords, how many gold ingots do you need?

12. You find 7 chests in each of 3 caves that you explore. How many chests do you find in all?

13. You make 3 towers. Each one is made of 10 blocks of obsidian. How many obsidian blocks do you use in all?

14. You stack 4 rows of 5 redstone ore blocks to build a wall. How many redstone ore blocks do you use in all?

15. A group of 4 skeletons attacks you. Each skeleton shoots 8 arrows at you. How many arrows do the skeletons shoot in all?

HARDCORE MODE

Steve, Alex, and a villager collect as many emeralds as possible. Steve only collects 3 emeralds. The villager collects 4 times as many emeralds as Steve. Alex collects the most. She collects 6 times as many emeralds as the villager.

How many emeralds does Alex collect?

PVP SHOWDOWN

Which player earned the most experience points today? Solve the equations in each column then add up the answers to determine the winner of this PVP showdown.

1.	7 x 6 =	6 x 8 =
2.	3 x 5 =	4 x 9 =
3.	8 x 4 =	6 x 2 =
4.	9 x 1 =	3 x 3 =
5.	4 x 7 =	9 x 6 =
6.	6 x 6 =	3 x 8 =
TOTAL POINTS	_____	_____

Circle the winner:

 ALEX    STEVE

MULTIPLYING ONE- AND TWO-DIGIT NUMBERS

Read the problem carefully. Use the pictures for extra help. Write the answer in the space provided.

1. You use 20 blocks of cobblestone to build a tower. How many blocks of cobblestone do you use to build 4 towers?

2. A player rides in the railcart 15 times a day. After 3 days, how many times does the player ride in the railcart?

3. There are 14 blacksmith villagers who have 3 emeralds each. How many emeralds do the Blacksmith villagers have in all?

4.

You tame 2 wolves a day for 16 days. How many wolves do you tame in all?

MULTIPLYING ONE- AND TWO-DIGIT NUMBERS

(continued from previous page)

5. 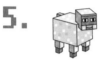 You have 4 farms with 17 sheep on each farm. How many sheep do you have in all?

6. You get 11 experience points from every creeper you kill. You kill 4 creepers. How many experience points do you get?

7. You mine 8 blocks of granite for 16 mornings straight. How many blocks do you mine in all?

8. You destroy 3 times more Endermen than zombie pigmen. You destroy 25 zombie pigmen. How many Endermen do you destroy?

9. Seven witches throw 26 splash potions in a day. How many splash potions do the witches throw in all?

10. 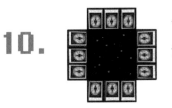 You see 4 groups of 16 Endermen when you enter the End. How many Endermen do you see in all?

11.  You tame 5 ocelots every time you enter the Jungle Biome. You enter the Jungle Biome 32 times. How many ocelots do you tame?

12. 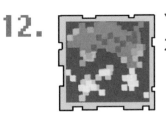 You use a map 8 times every time you play. If you play 22 times, how many times do you use a map?

MULTIPLYING ONE- AND TWO-DIGIT NUMBERS

(continued from previous page)

13.  You need 3 lapis lazuli to craft each enchanted bow and arrow. How many lapis lazuli do you need to make 19 enchanted bow and arrows?

14. 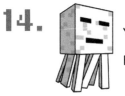 You destroy 15 ghasts in 8 minutes. If you continue at that rate, how many ghasts will you destroy in 24 minutes?

15.  A skeleton shoots 7 arrows at each villager he sees. He sees 29 villagers. How many arrows does he shoot?

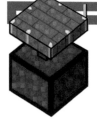

HARDCORE MODE

There are 14 desert temples. Each one has 10 active traps. You deactivate 14 of the traps by breaking the pressure plate. How many active traps are left?

PVP SHOWDOWN

Which player earned the most experience points today? Solve the equations in each column then add up the answers to determine the winner of this PVP showdown.

1.	12 x 6 =	10 x 8 =
2.	3 x 50 =	14 x 9 =
3.	11 x 4 =	16 x 2 =
4.	19 x 1 =	3 x 13 =
5.	24 x 2 =	15 x 6 =
6.	6 x 13 =	12 x 8 =

TOTAL POINTS _____   _____

Circle the winner:

ALEX   STEVE

DIVISION WITH 1- AND 2-DIGIT NUMBERS

Read the problem carefully. Use the pictures for extra help. Write the answer in the space provided.

1. You catch 9 fish with your fishing rod. You divide the fish among 3 cats. How many fish does each cat get?

2. There are 8 bats in 4 dungeons. If each dungeon has the same number of bats, how many bats are in each one?

3. There are 6 villagers. If each house in the village can fit 3 villagers, how many houses do they need?

4.  You have 4 diamond swords. You store 1 sword in each chest you own. How many chests do you own?

5. You have 15 skeleton spawn eggs. You sort them into 5 equal groups. How many eggs are in each group?

6. You make 3 identical walls out of 12 blocks of sandstone. How many blocks of sandstone do you use for each wall?

7. You have 18 diamonds. You give 6 of them to each villager you see until you're all out of diamonds. How many villagers did you see?

8. You have 16 blocks of wool in 4 different colors: blue, pink, lime, and yellow. If you have the same amount of every color, how many blocks do you have in each color?

DIVISION WITH 1- AND 2-DIGIT NUMBERS
(continued from previous page)

9. You approach a monster spawner in an Overworld dungeon. It spawns 20 monsters in all. If it spawns 5 of each kind of monster, how many kinds of monsters does it spawn?

10. You have 12 Ender eye pearls in your inventory. You place an equal amount in two different chests. How many Ender eye pearls do you place in each chest?

11. You battle the Ender Dragon a total of 16 times. Half of those times, you win. How many times do you win?

12. You earn 24 experience orbs for destroying a group of zombies. If every zombie you destroy earns you 6 experience orbs, how many zombies did you destroy?

13. You start your game with 20 bones. You need 2 bones to tame every wolf. How many wolves can you tame?

14. You battle 24 ghasts in the Nether. If you destroy 3 ghasts a minute, how many minutes does it take to destroy all of the ghasts?

15. A player has 10 hearts. He loses 1 heart every time he runs into a zombie. How many zombies can he run into before he's out of hearts?

HARDCORE MODE

You craft 27 tools and 6 pieces of armor. You place all of these items in 3 different chests for safe keeping. If you have an equal amount of items in all 3 chests, how many items are stored in each chest?

PVP SHOWDOWN

Which player earned the most experience points today? Solve the equations in each column then add up the answers to determine the winner of this PVP showdown.

1.	12 ÷ 6 =	16 ÷ 8 =
2.	15 ÷ 3 =	9 ÷ 3 =
3.	12 ÷ 4 =	18 ÷ 2 =
4.	20 ÷ 5 =	14 ÷ 7 =
5.	49 ÷ 7 =	42 ÷ 6 =
6.	16 ÷ 4 =	18 ÷ 3 =

TOTAL POINTS _____   _____

Circle the winner:

 ALEX    STEVE

DIVISION WITH 1- AND 2-DIGIT NUMBERS

(continued)

1. You need 12 Eyes of Ender to activate an End portal. You get 4 Eyes of Ender from every villager you trade with. How many villagers do you need to trade with to have enough Eyes of Ender to activate the End portal?

2. If each bowl of mushroom stew restores 2 hunger points, how many bowls do you need to eat to restore 24 hunger points?

3. 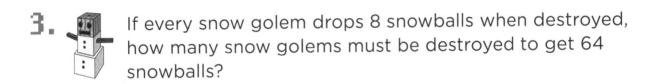 If every snow golem drops 8 snowballs when destroyed, how many snow golems must be destroyed to get 64 snowballs?

4. If you can craft 9 boats a week using your resources, how many weeks will it take to craft 27 boats?

DIVISION WITH 1- AND 2-DIGIT NUMBERS

(continued from previous page)

5.  There are 63 apples in your inventory today. Each horse on your farm needs to be fed 7 apples. How many horses can you feed?

6.  To brew 4 potions of Water Breathing, you need 32 pufferfish. How many pufferfish do you need to make 1 potion of Water Breathing?

7. 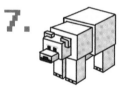 Every polar bear drops 6 fish when destroyed. If you need 36 fish, how many polar bears do you need to destroy?

8. You craft 5 jack-o-lanterns every day. If you have 35 jack-o-lanterns, how many days did you spend crafting them?

9.  Your farm has 42 cows. You divide them equally among 7 farms. How many cows do you keep on each farm?

10.  You encounter 54 creepers. You destroy 9 of them with each block of TNT you use. How many TNT blocks do you need to destroy all of the creepers?

11.  It takes you 81 minutes to craft 9 houses. How many minutes would you estimate it takes to craft each house?

12. 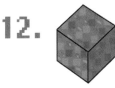 Your cobblestone house has 20 windows. It has the same number of windows on all 4 walls of the house. How many windows does it have on each wall?

DIVISION WITH 1- AND 2-DIGIT NUMBERS

(continued from previous page)

13. Every time you enter the Nether fortress, you battle 3 wither skeletons. If you battle 36 wither skeletons, how many times did you enter the Nether fortress?

14. You place 8 rows of grass blocks. You use 32 grass blocks in all. How many grass blocks did you place in each row?

15. You use your enchantment table to enchant 56 swords and shovels. You enchant 7 items at a time. How many groups of items do you enchant?

HARDCORE MODE

A group of blazes in the Nether fortress shoots 54 fireballs at you. You dodge all of them. Another group of blazes shoot an additional 21 fireballs at you. You are hit by 12 of them. If each blaze can only shoot 3 fireballs, how many blazes did you battle?

PVP SHOWDOWN

Which player earned the most experience points today? Solve the equations in each column then add up the answers to determine the winner of this PVP showdown.

1.	81 ÷ 9 =	64 ÷ 8 =
2.	30 ÷ 5 =	24 ÷ 4 =
3.	92 ÷ 4 =	60 ÷ 5 =
4.	36 ÷ 2 =	56 ÷ 8 =
5.	40 ÷ 8 =	42 ÷ 6 =
6.	21 ÷ 3 =	55 ÷ 11 =

TOTAL POINTS _____   _____

Circle the winner:

ALEX   STEVE

DIVISION WITH 1- AND 2-DIGIT NUMBERS

(continued from previous page)
Read the problem carefully. Use the pictures for extra help.
Write the answer in the space provided.

1. You start a game with 34 hunger points. Every time you build a shelter, you lose 2 hunger points. How many shelters can you build before you lose all of your hunger points?

2.  You swing your sword 68 times, but it takes 17 swings to destroy each zombie. How many zombies can you destroy?

3. Your wolves destroy a total of 64 creepers in the Overworld. If each of your wolves destroyed 4 creepers, how many wolves do you have?

4.  Squids drop 72 ink sacs into the water. You dive down to collect them, but you have to come up for air every time you collect 8 ink sacs. How many times do you come up for air as you collect all of the ink sacs?

5. You have 85 minutes until nightfall. It takes you 5 minutes to build a shelter. How many shelters can you build before nightfall?

6. You have 49 empty buckets. You put them into groups of 7 to fill with milk. How many groups of buckets do you have?

7. There are 90 ocelots in the Jungle Biome. A group of 5 ocelots is enough to scare away 1 creeper. How many creepers can all of the ocelots scare away?

8.  You want to craft 2 equally sized beacons using 56 blocks. How many blocks will you use for each beacon?

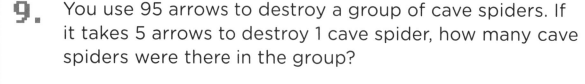

(continued from previous page)

9. You use 95 arrows to destroy a group of cave spiders. If it takes 5 arrows to destroy 1 cave spider, how many cave spiders were there in the group?

10. A group of creepers drops 44 units of gunpowder. Each creeper drops 2 units of gunpowder. How many creepers are in the group?

11. You find 76 cobwebs in an abandoned mineshaft. With each snip of your shears, you collect 4 cobwebs. How many snips does it take to collect all of the cobwebs?

12. A group of zombie pigmen drops 63 pieces of rotten flesh. If each zombie pigman drops 3 pieces of rotten flesh, how many zombie pigman are in the group?

13. A ghast hurls 81 fireballs at you and hits you every time. You die and respawn after being hit by 9 of them. How many times do you die and respawn?

14. You have 75 spawn eggs in your inventory. You use 15 of them every time you play. How many times do you play before running out of spawn eggs?

15. You are trying to build a 54-step staircase out of sandstone blocks. You stop after every 9 blocks to rest and eat something. How many times do you stop?

HARDCORE MODE
If each of a wither's 3 heads spit 18 skulls at you during a battle and you take damage every time 6 skulls are spit at you, how many times do you take damage?

PVP SHOWDOWN

Which player earned the most experience points today? Solve the equations in each column then add up the answers to determine the winner of this PVP showdown.

1. $96 \div 6 =$ $\qquad$ $76 \div 2 =$

2. $45 \div 5 =$ $\qquad$ $44 \div 11 =$

3. $68 \div 4 =$ $\qquad$ $16 \div 2 =$

4. $9 \div 1 =$ $\qquad$ $33 \div 3 =$

5. $14 \div 7 =$ $\qquad$ $81 \div 9 =$

6. $64 \div 2 =$ $\qquad$ $21 \div 7 =$

TOTAL POINTS _____ _____

Circle the winner:

 ALEX    STEVE

26

MULTIPLYING AND DIVIDING WITHIN 100

Read the problem carefully. Use the pictures for extra help. Write the answer in the space provided.

1. You ride the minecart rail 2 times a day for 34 days. How many times do you ride the minecart rail?

2. You want to transport 36 chests to your base, but you can only transport 4 chests at a time. How many times do you need to transport groups of chests?

3. 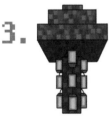 You visit the Desert Biome 12 times more often than the Jungle Biome. If you visit the Jungle Biome 3 times, how many times do you visit the Desert Biome?

4. You have 49 splash potions. You need 7 splash potions to cure each zombie villager. How many zombie villagers can you cure?

5. You use your new saddle to ride 7 groups of 6 pigs. How many pigs do you ride in all?

6. You collect 76 pieces of raw beef after destroying a group of mooshrooms. If each mooshroom drops 4 pieces of raw beef, how many mooshrooms did you destroy?

7. You drink 4 potions of Swiftness and 8 times as many potions of Strength. How many potions of Strength did you drink?

8. You visit the End 55 times. Every 5 times you visit, you find Elytra! How many times do you find Elytra?

9.  An iron golem drops 35 red flowers. A group of 7 villagers divides the flowers equally between themselves. How many flowers does each villager get?

10. 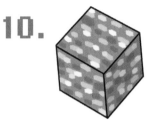 You want to mine 60 layers of diamond ore. If your pickaxe breaks after every 12 layers, how many times does your pickaxe break?

11.  You place 12 rows of 7 lapis lazuli ore blocks. How many lapis lazuli ore blocks do you place in all?

12. 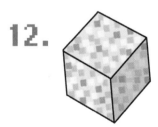 You place 30 iron blocks in 6 equal rows. How many iron blocks are in each row?

MULTIPLYING AND DIVIDING WITHIN 100

(continued from previous page)

13. You gather 21 ingredients to make a potion. You need 3 ingredients to make each bottle of potion. How many bottles of potion can you make?

14. You chop down a total of 63 trees. You build 7 beds from all of the wood. How many trees make a bed?

15. You destroy 10 mobs in one day in Survival mode. You destroy 8 times as many mobs the next day. How many mobs do you destroy the next day?

HARDCORE MODE

You want to make 23 cakes. Each one requires 3 milk and 2 sugar. You have 64 milk and 40 sugar. How much more do you need of each ingredient?

PVP SHOWDOWN

Which player earned the most experience points today?
Solve the equations in each column then add up the
answers to determine the winner of this PVP showdown.

1.	27 ÷ 3 =	8 x 1 =
2.	45 ÷ 5 =	4 x 3 =
3.	8 x 5 =	6 ÷ 2 =
4.	14 ÷ 2 =	21 ÷ 3 =
5.	34 ÷ 17 =	3 x 9 =
6.	6 x 4 =	42 ÷ 6 =

TOTAL POINTS _____   _____

Circle the winner:

ALEX   STEVE

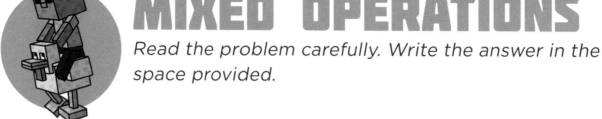

MIXED OPERATIONS

Read the problem carefully. Write the answer in the space provided.

1. 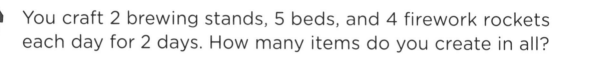 You craft 2 brewing stands, 5 beds, and 4 firework rockets each day for 2 days. How many items do you create in all?

2.  Over 4 days, you destroy 6 hostile mobs and 2 neutral mobs. If you destroy the same number of mobs each day, how many mobs do you destroy each day?

3. You have 4 diamonds in each of 8 chests. You collect 10 more diamonds while mining. How many diamonds do you have in all?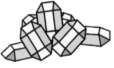

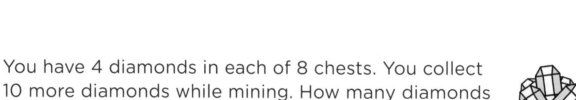

4. 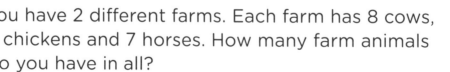 You have 2 different farms. Each farm has 8 cows, 3 chickens and 7 horses. How many farm animals do you have in all?

5. There are 7 groups of 4 zombies approaching you. You destroy 16 zombies. How many zombies are left?

6.  You offer 9 emeralds to the first 3 villagers you meet and 6 emeralds to the next 4 villagers. How many emeralds do you offer for trade?

7. You build 8 beacons every day for 3 days. You build 12 beacons the next day. How many beacons do you build in all?

8.  You place 8 minecart rails in the morning and 5 times that amount in the afternoon. Creepers blow up half of the rails. How many rails are left?

MIXED OPERATIONS

(continued from previous page)

9. You battle 8 skeletons and 4 zombies one day and 2 groups of 3 creepers the next day. How many mobs do you battle in all?

10.  You enchant 13 books and 4 swords every day for 2 days. You break 2 of the swords. How many enchanted items do you still have?

11. You shoot 7 arrows at a creeper and twice as many arrows at a giant zombie. Only 7 of them hit their target. How many arrows do not hit their target?

12. You see 6 groups of 5 creepers approaching. Before they get near you, 4 creepers explode. How many creepers are left?

13. Two witches each throw 3 potions of Slowness, 9 potions of Weakness, and 2 potions of Poison. How many potions are thrown in all?

14. You tame 7 groups of 5 ocelots and 3 groups of 6 horses. How many animals do you tame in all?

15. The Ender Dragon fires 4 Ender charges at you every time you enter the End. You enter the End 16 times one day and 5 times the next. How many Ender charges does the Ender Dragon fire in all?

HARDCORE MODE

You battle 16 ghasts and destroy half of them. The ones you destroy drop a variety of items. Half of them drop 2 gunpowder and the other half drop one ghast tear. How many items are dropped in all?

PVP SHOWDOWN

Which player earned the most experience points today? Solve the equations in each column then add up the answers to determine the winner of this PVP showdown.

1.	18 ÷ 9 =	6 + 8 =
2.	7 - 5 =	4 x 4 =
3.	9 + 4 =	6 ÷ 2 =
4.	5 x 1 =	3 - 3 =
5.	8 x 7 =	9 + 6 =
6.	16 ÷ 4 =	3 x 8 =

TOTAL POINTS _____ _____

Circle the winner:

 ALEX    STEVE

DIVISION WITH REMAINDERS

Read the problem carefully. Use the pictures for extra help. Write the answer in the space provided.

1. You have 43 experience points. You need 4 experience points to enchant a bow and arrow. How many bow and arrows can you enchant, and how many experience points will you have left over?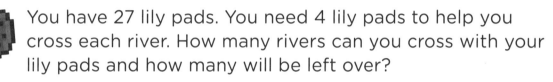

2.  You have 27 lily pads. You need 4 lily pads to help you cross each river. How many rivers can you cross with your lily pads and how many will be left over?

3. You plant 18 cactus blocks on your farm in rows of 5. How many rows do you plant, and how many blocks are left over?

4. You place 35 items in equal amounts in 4 different chests. How many items are in each chest and how many are left over?

DIVISION WITH REMAINDERS

(continued from previous page)

5. You trade with 7 different villagers in 44 minutes. If it takes the same amount of time to trade with each villager, how much time do you spend trading with each villager? How much time is left over after you've traded with all of them?

6. You have 67 snowballs and want to make as many snow golems as you can. You need 8 snowballs to make every snow golem. How many snow golems can you make, and how many snowballs will you have left over?

7. It takes 6 swings of your axe to chop down every spruce tree. If you only have enough durability to swing your axe 58 times, how many trees can you chop down, and how many swings could you still take?

8. You collect 87 Ender pearls after battling a group of Endermen. You need 4 Ender pearls to make one Eye of Ender. How many Eyes of Ender can you make, and how many Ender pearls will be left over?

MULTIPLICATION AND DIVISION OF 2- AND 3-DIGIT NUMBERS

Read the problem carefully. Use the pictures for extra help. Write the answer in the space provided.

1. You have 27 coal blocks to use in your furnace. If each block of coal can smelt 80 items, how many items can you smelt?

2.  You have 150 zombie eggs in your inventory. You use 15 of those eggs every day to spawn zombies. How many days pass before you run out of zombie eggs?

3.  You lose 18 hunger points from exhaustion every day over 23 days of mining. How many hunger points do you lose over all 23 days?

4. 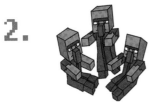 You brew 217 potions of Weakness. You need 7 potions to heal every zombie villager you meet. How many zombie villagers can you heal?

(continued from previous page)

5. You get 230 experience points from battling 5 skeletons. How many experience points do you estimate you get for battling each skeleton?

6. You have 196 wood planks. You need 7 wood planks to craft a boat. How many boats can you craft from all of your wood planks?

7. There are 122 donkeys total in the Plains Biome. If you bred them and tripled the number of donkeys in the Plains Biome, how many donkeys would there be?

HARDCORE MODE

Your dad says you can have 35 minutes of gaming time on every school day and 45 minutes of gaming time on each weekend day. Your mom says you can have 25 minutes of gaming time on every school day and 60 minutes on each weekend day. Which parent is offering you the most gaming time per week?

PVP SHOWDOWN

Which player earned the most experience points today? Solve the equations in each column then add up the answers to determine the winner of this PVP showdown.

1.	$425 \div 5 =$	$126 \div 6 =$
2.	$315 \div 5 =$	$44 \div 4 =$
3.	$28 \times 2 =$	$62 \div 2 =$
4.	$8 \times 2 =$	$42 \div 6 =$
5.	$14 \div 7 =$	$19 \div 1 =$
6.	$16 \times 6 =$	$3 \times 44 =$

TOTAL POINTS _____   _____

Circle the winner:

ALEX   STEVE

ADDING AND SUBTRACTING FRACTIONS

Solve the equations and simplify your answers.

1.  You are attacked by a group of Endermen. You destroy $\frac{1}{4}$ of them with your sword and $\frac{2}{4}$ of them with your bow and arrow. What fraction of the Endermen did you destroy?

2. You battle a group of ghasts in the Nether. While you're battling, $\frac{1}{6}$ of their fireballs miss you and $\frac{4}{6}$ of them are deflected by your shield. The rest inflict damage. What fraction of fireballs inflict damage?

3.  You build $\frac{4}{8}$ of your cobblestone structure one day and $\frac{2}{8}$ of it the next day. What fraction of your cobblestone structure have you built in all?

4.  You use golden apples to cure $\frac{1}{16}$ of a group of zombie villagers. You craft a few more golden apples and cure another $\frac{4}{16}$ of the zombie villagers. What fraction of villagers have not been cured?

5. An iron golem destroys $\frac{1}{12}$ of a group of zombies. You destroy $\frac{3}{12}$ of the zombies. What fraction of the zombies are destroyed?

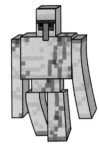

6. You use $\frac{3}{9}$ of your weapons in battle and $\frac{1}{9}$ of your weapons to mine valuable resources. What fraction of your weapons are still unused?

7. You use your brewing stand to brew a bunch of potions. You use $\frac{1}{5}$ of the potions on blazes, $\frac{1}{5}$ on wither skeletons, and $\frac{1}{5}$ on zombie pigmen. What fraction of your potions do you use?

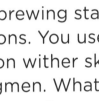

8. You enchant your armor for added protection. You enchant $\frac{3}{7}$ of your armor the first day and $\frac{3}{7}$ of your armor the next day. What fraction of your armor is not enchanted?

ADDING AND SUBTRACTING FRACTIONS WITH DIFFERENT DENOMINATORS

Make the fractions equivalent. Then add them or subtract them. Simplify your answers.

1. You battle a group of hostile mobs. If $\frac{1}{6}$ of the hostile mobs fall in a lava pit and $\frac{3}{12}$ are destroyed by your arrows, what fraction of hostile mobs remain?

2. You use $\frac{1}{9}$ of your gold ingots to make a clock and $\frac{2}{3}$ of your gold ingots to make weapons. What fraction of your gold ingots do you use in all?

3. You use $\frac{1}{4}$ of your wooden sticks to make garden hoes. You use $\frac{1}{3}$ of your wooden sticks to make arrows. What fraction of your wooden sticks remains?

4. 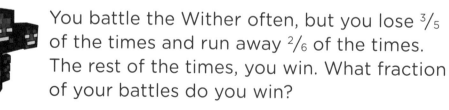 You battle the Wither often, but you lose $\frac{3}{5}$ of the times and run away $\frac{2}{6}$ of the times. The rest of the times, you win. What fraction of your battles do you win?

5.  You used ⁴/₇ of your diamonds to make armor and ¹/₃ of them to make weapons. What fraction of your diamonds did you use in all?

6. Your inventory is getting full. You know that ¹/₅ of your inventory is food, ¹/₄ of it is tools, and ¹/₂₀ of it is building materials. What fraction of your inventory is none of these things?

7. If you eat ⁴/₁₀ of your fish and use ²/₅ of your fish to tame ocelots, what fraction of your fish do you use in all?

HARDCORE MODE

Write your own word problem with fractions below and show it to your friend, your teacher, or your parent. Challenge him or her to solve it!

_____

_____

_____

_____

PVP SHOWDOWN

Which player earned the most experience points today? Solve the equations in each column then add up the answers to determine the winner of this PVP showdown.

1. $^1/_8 + {}^2/_8 =$ $^1/_6 + {}^2/_6 =$

2. $^1/_4 + {}^1/_4 =$ $^3/_6 + {}^2/_6 =$

3. $^3/_8 + {}^4/_8 =$ $^2/_6 + {}^2/_6 =$

4. $^3/_8 + {}^1/_8 =$ $^1/_3 + {}^1/_3 =$

5. $^4/_4 + {}^6/_4 =$ $^9/_6 + {}^8/_6 =$

TOTAL POINTS _____   _____

Circle the winner:

 ALEX    STEVE

MULTIPLYING FRACTIONS BY A WHOLE NUMBER

Multiply and write the answer. Fractions should be written in their simplest form.

1. You battle 3 times against an army of husks using ⅙ of your weapons each time you battle. What fraction of your weapons do you use over the course of the battles?

2. You build 7 towers. Each time you build a tower, you use 1/8 of your gold ore. ⅛ gold ore. What fraction of your gold ore do you use in all?

3. You destroy ⅔ the amount of spiders that your friend destroys. If your friend destroys 15 spiders, how many do you destroy?

4. Today you catch ⅔ the amount of pufferfish that you caught yesterday. If you caught 6 pufferfish yesterday, how many do you catch today?

MULTIPLYING FRACTIONS BY A WHOLE NUMBER

(continued from previous page)

5. 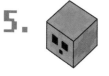 You are attacked by 20 slimes one night and $\frac{3}{10}$ the amount of slimes the next night. How many slimes attacked you the second time?

6.  You and your tamed wolf battle a group of 15 endermites. Your wolf destroys $\frac{1}{5}$ of them and leaves the rest for you to battle. How many endermites do you battle?

7. 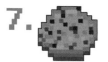 You eat a bunch of cookies and gain $\frac{1}{8}$ of your 16 hunger points back. How many hunger points do you gain?

8.  In the course of a day, $\frac{1}{6}$ of the 48 witches you battle drop spider eyes. How many witches drop spider eyes?

9. You craft ²/₅ of your 75 houses with lapis lazuli ore. How many houses are made of lapis lazuli ore?

10. You spawn 54 creepers on your mob farm your first day of gaming and ¹/₃ the amount of creepers the second day. How many creepers do you spawn the second day?

11. You destroy a group of chickens and collect 72 feathers. You use ¹/₁₂ of the feathers to make arrows. How many feathers do you use?

12. You come across 42 spider webs and snip ¹/₇ of them down with your shears. How many webs do you snip?

MULTIPLYING FRACTIONS BY A WHOLE NUMBER

(continued from previous page)

13. 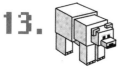 You see 74 animals in the Ice Plains Biome. You determine that ½ of them are polar bears. How many of them are polar bears?

14.  You grow 81 flowers on your farm and ⅑ that amount of flowers in a field. How many flowers do you grow in a field?

15.  You travel a distance of 40 blocks. You are wearing your Elytra wings for ⅕ of that journey. How many blocks do you travel wearing Elytra?

HARDCORE MODE

You eat 2½ cakes each day for 5 mornings to restore hunger points before a big day of mining. Over the next 4 days, you eat ½ of a cake each morning. How much cake do you eat over these 9 days?

PVP SHOWDOWN

Which player earned the most experience points today?
Solve the equations in each column then add up the
answers to determine the winner of this PVP showdown.

1. $\frac{1}{3} \times 6 =$ $8 \times \frac{2}{4} =$

2. $\frac{3}{5} \times 5 =$ $\frac{2}{3} \times 9 =$

3. $\frac{3}{4} \times 4 =$ $5 \times \frac{1}{5} =$

4. $\frac{1}{10} \times 5 =$ $3 \times \frac{2}{3} =$

5. $21 \times \frac{1}{7} =$ $\frac{2}{6} \times 6 =$

6. $8 \times \frac{1}{2} =$ $7 \times \frac{1}{7} =$

TOTAL POINTS _____   _____

Circle the winner:

ALEX   STEVE

SOLVING FOR AREA

Use the equation provided to determine the area.

Area = length x width

1. Your farm is 8 feet long and 4 feet wide. What is the area of your farm?

2. You plant saplings on a section of grass that is 6 feet long and 5 feet wide. What is the area of your sapling farm?

3. The village library is 6 feet wide and 4 feet long. What is the area of the village library?

4. You discover a layer of redstone ore that is 8 feet long and 4 feet wide. What is the area of the layer?

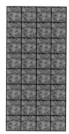

5. A skeleton patrols an area of the Nether fortress that is 9 feet long and 9 feet wide. What is the area of this section of the Nether fortress?

6. A pig will turn into a zombie pigman if lightning strikes anywhere inside his 4-foot-long, 4-foot-wide fenced area. What is the area inside the fence?

7. You mine a section of obsidian that is 4 feet long and 9 feet wide. What is the area of the obsidian?

8. A zombie falls in a pit that is 7 feet long by 6 feet wide. What is the area of the lava pit?

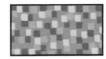

SOLVING FOR PERIMETER

You can find the perimeter of a 2-dimensional shape by adding all of its sides. Use the equations on the signs to help you solve these word problems.

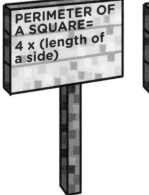

PERIMETER OF A SQUARE=
4 x (length of a side)

PERIMETER OF A RECTANGLE=
(2 x length) + (2 x width)

9. A creeper explodes and leaves a square opening in the ground that is 4 feet long. What is the perimeter of the opening?

10. 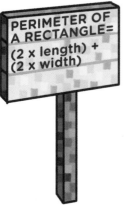 A zombie walks the edges of a rectangular shelter, trying to find an entrance. The shelter is 5 feet long and 7 feet wide. What is the perimeter of the shelter?

11.  You water a melon farm that is 8 feet long and 13 feet wide. What is the perimeter of the melon farm?

HARDCORE MODE

You know that the perimeter of a square desert temple room is 36 feet. You walk into another desert temple room with a perimeter that is double the length of the first room. How long is each wall in room 1? How long is each wall in room 2?

PVP SHOWDOWN

Which player's shelter has the greatest area? Solve the equations in each column to find the area of each room of their shelters and then add up the area of each room to determine the winner of this PVP showdown.

1.	7 ft. x 9 ft. =	7 ft. x 8 ft. =
2.	5 ft. x 5 ft. =	4 ft. x 6 ft. =
3.	3 ft. x 4 ft. =	5 ft. x 2 ft. =
4.	7 ft. x 2 ft. =	3 ft. x 3 ft. =
5.	5 ft. x 7 ft. =	9 ft. x 7 ft. =
6.	3 ft. x 6 ft. =	2 ft. x 8 ft. =

TOTAL SQUARE FOOTAGE _____   _____

Circle the winner:

 ALEX    STEVE

55

SOLVING FOR AREA AND PERIMETER

Use the formulas you've learned to solve for area or perimeter.

1. 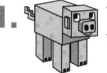 You keep your pigs in a pen that is 12 feet long and 5 feet wide. What is the area of the pig pen?

2. You surround a valuable chest with a square border of TNT. Your TNT border is 15 feet long. What is the perimeter of your TNT border?

3. You are trying to stay alive during a battle with a ghast. The danger zone where a ghast's fireballs can reach you is shaped like a rectangle. It's 17 feet long and 6 feet wide. What is the area of this danger zone?

4.  You want to build a rail system along the edges of a rectangular field that is 13 feet long and 10 feet wide. How many feet of rails do you need?

5. The square foundation of your cobblestone and wood house is 81 square feet. What is the length of one side of the foundation?

6. You want to avoid getting hit by a witch's splash potions. The rectangular splash zone is 8 feet long and 20 feet wide. What is the area of the witch's splash zone?

7. You harvest wheat on a farm that is 13 feet long and 7 feet wide. What is the area of your wheat farm?

8. A square end portal is 6 feet on every side. What is the perimeter of the end portal?

PVP ULTIMATE SHOWDOWN

Here is your final math challenge:
Go back and look at your calculations to see which avatar (Steve or Alex) won the most PVP battles. Circle the winner below.

With the help of your winning avatar and all of the experience points you've earned by practicing word problems, you've conquered the two boss mobs below.

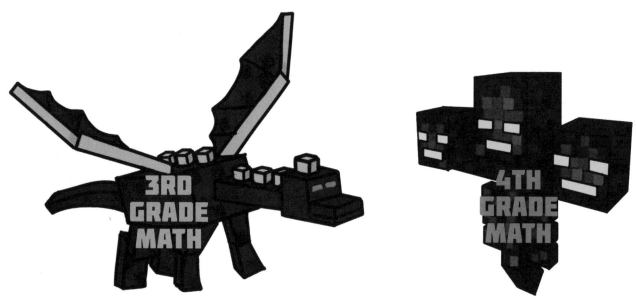

CONGRATULATIONS AND HAPPY MATH ADVENTURES!

ANSWER KEY

PAGE 2
1. 56 arrows
2. 24 silverfish
3. 16 fireballs
4. 30 unit of gunpowder

PAGE 3
5. 28 damage
6. 9 torches
7. 16 hearts
8. 27 swords

PAGE 4
9. 42 spiders
10. 15 pieces of rotten flesh
11. 16 gold ingots
12. 21 chests

PAGE 5
13. 30 obsidian blocks
14. 20 redstone ore blocks
15. 32 arrows
Hardcore mode
72 emeralds

PAGE 6
PVP Showdown
Alex: 162 experience points
Steve: 183 experience points

PAGE 7
1. 80 blocks
2. 45 times
3. 42 emeralds
4. 32 wolves

PAGE 8
5. 68 sheep
6. 44 experience points
7. 128 blocks
8. 75 Endermen

PAGE 9
9. 182 splash potions
10. 64 Endermen
11. 160 ocelots
12. 176 times

PAGE 10
13. 57 lapis lazuli
14. 45 ghasts
15. 203 arrows
Hardcore mode
126 active traps

PAGE 11
PVP Showdown
Alex: 411 experience points
Steve: 463 experience points

PAGE 12
1. 3 fish
2. 2 bats
3. 2 houses
4. 4 chests

PAGE 13
5. 3 eggs
6. 4 blocks
7. 3 villagers
8. 4 blocks

PAGE 14
9. 4 kinds
10. 6 Ender eye pearls
11. 8 times
12. 4 zombies

PAGE 15
13. 10 wolves
14. 8 minutes
15. 10 zombies
Hardcore mode
11 items

PAGE 16

PVP Showdown

Alex: 25 experience points

Steve: 29 experience points

PAGE 17

1. 3 villagers
2. 12 bowls
3. 8 snow golems
4. 3 weeks

PAGE 18

5. 9 horses
6. 8 pufferfish
7. 6 polar bears
8. 7 days

PAGE 19

9. 6 cows
10. 6 blocks
11. 9 minutes
12. 5 windows

PAGE 20

13. 12 times
14. 4 grass blocks
15. 8 groups of items

Hardcore mode

25 blazes

PAGE 21

PVP Showdown

Alex: 68 experience points

Steve: 45 experience points

PAGE 22

1. 17 shelters
2. 4 zombies
3. 16 tamed wolves
4. 9 times

PAGE 23

5. 17 shelters
6. 7 groups
7. 18 creepers
8. 28 blocks

PAGE 24

9. 19 cave spiders
10. 22 creepers
11. 19 snips
12. 21 zombie pigmen

PAGE 25

13. 9 times
14. 5 times
15. 6 times

Hardcore mode

9 times

PAGE 26

PVP Showdown

Alex: 85

Steve: 73

PAGE 27

1. 68 times
2. 9 times
3. 36 times
4. 7 zombie villagers

PAGE 28

5. 42 pigs
6. 19 mooshrooms
7. 32 potions of Strength
8. 11 times

PAGE 29

9. 5 flowers
10. 5 times
11. 84 lapis lazuli ore
12. 5 iron blocks

PAGE 30

13. 7 bottles
14. 9 trees
15. 80 mobs

Hardcore mode

5 milk, 6 sugar

PAGE 31

PVP Showdown

Alex: 91   Steve: 64

PAGE 32

1. 22 items
2. 2 mobs
3. 42 diamonds
4. 36 farm animals

PAGE 33

5. 12 zombies
6. 51 emeralds
7. 36 beacons
8. 24 rails

PAGE 34

9. 18 mobs
10. 32 enchanted items
11. 14 arrows
12. 26 creepers

PAGE 35

13. 28 potions
14. 53 animals
15. 84 Ender charges

Hardcore mode

12 items

PAGE 36

PVP Showdown

Alex: 82   Steve: 72

PAGE 37

1. 10 bow and arrows, 3 left over
2. 6 rivers, 3 lily pads left over
3. 3 rows, 3 cactuses left over
4. 8 items, 3 items left over

PAGE 38

5. 6 minutes, 2 minutes left over
6. 8 snow golems, 3 snowballs left over
7. 9 trees, 4 swings
8. 21 Eye of Ender, 3 Ender pearls left over

PAGE 39

1. 2,160 items
2. 10 days
3. 414 hunger points
4. 31 zombie villagers

PAGE 40

5. 46 experience points.
6. 28 boats
7. 366 donkeys

Hardcore mode

Dad: 265   Mom: 245 minutes

PAGE 41

PVP Showdown

Alex: 318   Steve: 221

PAGE 42

1. $3/4$ of the Endermen
2. $1/6$ of the fireballs inflict damage
3. $3/4$ of the cobblestone structure
4. $11/16$ of the villagers

PAGE 43

5. $1/3$ of the zombies
6. $5/9$ of your weapons
7. $3/5$ of your potions
8. $1/7$ of your armor

PAGE 44

1. $7/12$ of the hostile mobs remain
2. $7/9$ of your gold ingots
3. $5/12$ of your wooden sticks
4. $1/15$ of your battles

PAGE 45

5. $19/21$ of your diamonds
6. $1/2$ of your inventory
7. $4/5$ of your fish

PAGE 46

PVP Showdown

Alex: $38/8 = 4 3/4$ **Steve: $33/6 = 5 1/2$**

Hardcore mode

Answer may vary

PAGE 47

1. $\frac{1}{2}$ of your weapons
2. $\frac{7}{8}$ of the towers are gold ore
3. 10 spiders
4. 4 pufferfish

PAGE 48

5. 6 slimes
6. 12 endermites
7. 2 hunger points
8. 8 witches

PAGE 49

9. 30 houses
10. 18 creepers
11. 6 feathers
12. 6 webs

PAGE 50

13. 37 are polar bears
14. 9 flowers
15. 8 blocks

Hardcore mode

$14\frac{1}{2}$ cakes

PAGE 51

PVP Showdown
Alex: 15 1/2   **Steve: 16**

PAGE 52

1. 32 square feet
2. 30 square feet
3. 24 square feet
4. 32 square feet

PAGE 53

5. 81 square feet
6. 16 square feet
7. 36 square feet
8. 42 square feet

PAGE 54

9. 16 feet
10. 24 feet
11. 42 feet

Hardcore mode

room 1: 9 feet long   room 2: 18 feet long

PAGE 55

PVP Showdown
Alex: 167 square feet   **Steve: 178 square feet**

PAGE 56

1. 60 square feet
2. 60 feet
3. 102 square feet
4. 46 feet

PAGE 57

5. 9 feet
6. 160 square feet
7. 91 square feet
8. 24 feet

PAGE 58

Steve (6 wins)   Alex (5 wins)